Cool Hotels
Italy

teNeues

Imprint

Produced by fusion publishing GmbH, Stuttgart . Los Angeles   www.fusion-publishing.com

Editorial team: Martin Nicholas Kunz (Editor + Layout)
Bärbel Holzberg (Introduction), Jake Townsend ("What's special" texts)
Viviana Guastalla, Hanna Martin (Editorial coordination)
Sabine Scholz (Text coordination), Alphagriese (Translation coordination)
Dr. Elisabetta Sangirardi (Italian), Christine Grimm (US-English), Stéphanie Laloix (French), Juan Francisco Lopez (Spanish)
Jan Hausberg, Anke Scholz (Prepress + imaging)

Cover photo (location): Henri del Olmo (Byblos Art Hotel Villa Amistà)

Back cover photos from top to bottom (location): Tonino Mosconi (Falconara Charming House & Resort), Henri del Olmo (Byblos Art Hotel Villa Amistà), Marchi e Marchi (Hotel Carducci76), Gianluca Perticoni (Sixty Hotel), courtesy Aldrovandi Palace

Photos (location): courtesy Aldrovandi Palace; Domenico Bandiera (Hotel Carducci76 pp. 25–27); Davide Barasa (The Chedi Milan); Julia Bornefeld (Hotel Greif, p. 164); courtesy Boscolo Hotels (Aleph, Exedra, Granducato p. 182); courtesy Bulgari (Bulgari Hotel Milan); Carlo Valentini (Riva Lofts Florence); courtesy Castello del Nero Hotel & Spa; courtesy Continentale; Paolo Cusenza (Ca' Nigra Lagoon Resort); Dgnet www.dgnet.it (J.K. Place); Sebastian Doerk (Caol Ishka p. 147); Marilú Eustachio (Hotel Greif p. 165); Alberto Ferrero (UNA Hotel Bologna, UNA Hotel Vittoria); Natale De Fino (Caol Ishka pp. 148+150); courtesy Fontelunga (Villa Fontelunga); courtesy Fortyseven; Michelle Galindo (Casa della Palma pp. 103, 106+107); GP Briozzo (Town House Galleria); courtesy Hotel Monaco & Grand Canal; Moreno Maggi (St. George Roma); Marchi e Marchi (Hotel Carducci76 p. 24); Emanuela Marino (Caol Ishka p. 149); Manfred Alois Mayr (Hotel Greif pp. 166–167); Tonino Mosconi (La Coluccia, Spiagge Sanpietro Resort, Donnalucata Resort Sicily, Falconara Charming House & Resort, Santa Teresa Resort); Courtesy NH Hotels (NHow-Hotel); courtesy of Palazzo Arzaga Hotel Spa & Golf Resort; Henri del Olmo (Byblos Art Hotel Villa Amistà); Giulio Oriani (duoMo hotel & noMi club); Mauro Parmesani (La Sommità); Gianluca Perticoni (Sixty Hotel); Giovanna Piemonti e Beatrice Pediconi (Hotel de Russie p. 124); courtesy Starwood Hotels & Resorts (Cala di Volpe); courtesy Stein Hotels and Resorts (Casa Angelina); courtesy STRAF; courtesy The Gray; Jörg Tietje (Alle Meraviglie, Ca' Pozzo, Novecento, Oltre il Giardino, Townhouse 12 p. 92); courtesy Townhouse 12 (Townhouse 12 pp. 93–95); courtesy vigilius mountain resort
All other photos by Martin Nicholas Kunz

Price orientation: € < 200 EUR, €€ 201–350 EUR, €€€ 351–550 EUR, €€€€ > 551 EUR

Published by teNeues Publishing Group

teNeues Verlag GmbH + Co. KG	teNeues Publishing Company	teNeues Publishing UK Ltd.
Am Selder 37	16 West 22nd Street	P.O. Box 402
47906 Kempen, Germany	New York, NY 10010, USA	West Byfleet
Tel.: 0049-(0)2152-916-0	Tel.: 001-212-627-9090	KT14 7ZF, Great Britain
Fax: 0049-(0)2152-916-111	Fax: 001-212-627-9511	Tel.: 0044-1932-403509
E-mail: books@teneues.de		Fax: 0044-1932-403514

teNeues France S.A.R.L.
93, rue Bannier
45000 Orléans, France
Tel.: 0033-2-38541071
Fax: 0033-2-38625340

Press department: arehn@teneues.de
Tel.: 0049-(0)2152-916-202

www.teneues.com

ISBN: 978-3-8327-9234-3

© 2008 teNeues Verlag GmbH + Co. KG, Kempen

Printed in Italy

Bibliographic information published by Die Deutsche Bibliothek.
Die Deutsche Bibliothek lists this publication in the Deutsche Nationalbibliografie;
detailed bibliographic data is available in the Internet at http://dnb.ddb.de.

Contents   Page

Introduction   5

Introduzione

Intraprendere un viaggio in Italia significa molto di più di un inizio vacanza. Ogni volta traspare anche il desiderio di una differente gioia di vivere, di voglia di vivere mediterranea e di leggerezza. L'Italia è amata come probabilmente nessun'altra meta di viaggio. Immagini di paesaggi, come quella delle dolci colline della Toscana con i loro ulivi argentei e i marcati cipressi di colore scuro rendono dipendenti. Non è da meno la brusca natura selvaggia del sud, che nelle zone della Sardegna, Sicilia e Puglia pare quasi arcaica. Si potrebbe capitolare di fronte alla ricchezza inestimabile del patrimonio artistico del paese, se non fosse per questo comportamento disinvolto degli italiani, che convivono con grande naturalezza con le testimonianze della loro storia di più di duemila anni.

Gli hotel qui presentati rispecchiano questa eccitante convivenza – nelle metropoli Milano, Firenze e Roma, ma anche nelle regioni di campagna o sulle isole. Nel sud della Sicilia, per esempio, il barone Bordonaro ha costruito in vista del suo grandioso castello medioevale un hotel decisamente moderno, il *Falconara Charming Resort*, che presenta piccoli accenni alla caparbia fortezza sul mare. E nel *Castello del Nero*, una residenza nobile del XXII secolo tra Siena e Firenze si può dormire in suite lussuose, sotto affreschi originali.

In alto sugli scogli pieni di crepacci della costa amalfitana, dove soffia ancora un velo del glamour degli anni cinquanta, la *Casa Angelina*, bianca splendente, pone invece con la sua costruzione chiaramente cubistica un accento conforme ai tempi. Già la vista spettacolare dalla terrazza e la lobby sopra la costa vertiginosa e il mare Tirreno blu profondo vale un viaggio. Che gli hotel in Roma non debbano necessariamente essere cari è dimostrato dalla *Casa della Palma* e il *Daphne Inn*, due B&B che offrono un comfort accessibile in un ambiente di buon gusto, mentre l'inaugurazione del *Bulgari Hotel* di Milano, che soddisfa pienamente la sua fama di metropoli alla moda e di design, ha avuto l'effetto di una carica d'innesto, a cui hanno dato seguito hotel come il *NHow-Hotel*, *The Chedi Milan*, *The Gray* e lo *STRAF*. Quest'ultimo assomiglia ad una dichiarazione provocatoria dell'architetto e stilista Vincenzo de Cotiis, che ha usato materiali che si trovano normalmente soltanto nelle costruzioni industriali – e li ha presi per un hotel di lusso dietro alla facciata di un vecchio palazzo.

Bärbel Holzberg

Introduction

The start of a trip to Italy marks so much more than just the beginning of a vacation. It always has overtones of the desire for another experience of life, of the Mediterranean *joie de vivre* and lightness. Italy may be loved the most among tourist destinations. Scenery like the gently rolling hills of Tuscany with its silvery shimmering olive trees and striking dark cypresses is addictive. The same can be said of the rugged wildness of the south, which almost seems archaic in parts of Sardinia, Sicily, and Apulia. It would be tempting to surrender to the immense abundance of the country's art treasures if it wasn't for the casual attitude of the Italians, who find it quite normal to live with the witnesses of their more than two-thousand years of history.

The hotels presented here reflect this exciting coexistence—in metropolises like Milan, Florence, and Rome, as well as in the rural regions or on the islands. For example, Baron Bordonaro built a resolutely modern vacation hotel in the south of Sicily called the *Falconara Charming Resort* within view of his magnificent medieval *castello*. The resort has subtle allusions to the defiant fortress by the sea. And *Castello del Nero*, an aristocratic estate from the 12th century between Siena and Florence, invites guests to sleep beneath original frescoes in luxurious suites.

On the other hand, the dazzling white *Casa Angelina* with its clear cubistic structure creates a contemporary accent high on the cliffs of the rugged Amalfi coast with its lingering hint of 1950s glamour. It's worth the trip to see the spectacular view from the terrace and lobby across the steep coastline and the deep-blue Tyrrhenian Sea. *Casa della Palma* and the *Daphne Inn*, two B&Bs that offer affordable comfort in a stylish ambience, show that hotels in Rome don't have to be expensive. On the other end of the spectrum, the opening of the *Bulgari Hotel* in Milan—which more than does justice to its reputation as a fashion and design metropolis—had the effect of an initial spark that was followed by hotels like *NHow-Hotel*, *The Chedi Milan*, *The Gray*, and *STRAF*. The latter is like a provocative statement by the architect and fashion designer Vincenzo de Cotiis, who used materials that are normally just found in industrial buildings—for a luxury hotel behind the façade of an old *palazzo*.

Bärbel Holzberg

Einleitung

Der Antritt einer Italienreise markiert so viel mehr als den Beginn eines Urlaubs. Jedes Mal schwingt der Wunsch nach einem anderen Lebensgefühl mit, nach mediterraner Lebenslust und Leichtigkeit. Italien wird geliebt wie vielleicht kein anderes Reiseland. Landschaftsbilder, wie das der sanft geschwungenen Hügel der Toskana mit ihren silbrig flirrenden Olivenbäumen und markanten dunklen Zypressen machen süchtig. Nicht weniger die schroffe Wildheit des Südens, die in Teilen Sardiniens, Siziliens und Apuliens fast archaisch anmutet. Vor der unermesslichen Fülle an Kunstschätzen des Landes könnte man kapitulieren, wäre da nicht diese lässige Haltung der Italiener, die ganz selbstverständlich mit den Zeugen ihrer mehr als zweitausend Jahre alten Geschichte leben.

Die hier vorgestellten Hotels spiegeln dieses spannende Miteinander wider – in den Metropolen Mailand, Florenz und Rom, aber auch in den ländlichen Regionen oder auf den Inseln. Im Süden Siziliens beispielsweise hat Baron Bordonaro in Sichtweite seines grandiosen mittelalterlichen Castellos mit dem *Falconara Charming Resort* ein konsequent modernes Ferienhotel gebaut, mit subtilen Anspielungen auf die trutzige Burg am Meer. Und im *Castello del Nero*, einem Adelssitz aus dem 12. Jahrhundert zwischen Siena und Florenz, kann man in luxuriösen Suiten unter originalen Fresken schlafen.

Hoch auf den Klippen der zerklüfteten Amalfiküste, wo noch immer ein Hauch des Glamours der Fifties weht, setzt die blendend weiße *Casa Angelina* mit ihrem klaren kubistischen Bau hingegen einen zeitgemäßen Akzent. Allein der spektakuläre Ausblick von der Terrasse und Lobby aus über die Steilküste und das tiefblaue Tyrrhenische Meer ist eine Reise wert. Dass Hotels in Rom nicht teuer sein müssen, zeigen die *Casa della Palma* und das *Daphne Inn*, zwei B&Bs, die erschwinglichen Komfort in einem stylischen Ambiente bieten, während die Eröffnung des *Bulgari Hotels* in Mailand, das seinem Ruf als Mode- und Designmetropole darin mehr als gerecht wird, wie eine Initialzündung wirkte, der Hotels wie *NHow-Hotel*, *The Chedi Milan*, *The Gray* und *STRAF* folgten. Letzteres gleicht einem provokanten Statement des Architekten und Modedesigners Vincenzo de Cotiis, der Materialien verwendete, die man sonst nur in Industriebauten findet – und das für ein Luxushotel hinter der Fassade eines alten Palazzos.

Bärbel Holzberg

Introduction

Un départ pour l'Italie représente plus que le seul début des vacances. Il implique toujours le désir de vivre une autre expérience de vie, de connaître *la dolce vita* et la légèreté méditerranéennes. L'Italie est peut-être la destination la plus appréciée des voyageurs. Les paysages, comme ceux de Toscane, aux douces collines plantées d'oliviers aux reflets d'argent et de beaux cyprès sombres, créent une véritable dépendance, tout comme ceux des régions escarpées et sauvages du sud, qui peuvent parfois revêtir une apparence archaïque en Sardaigne, en Sicile et dans les Pouilles. On pourrait être tenté d'abandonner devant l'abondance d'œuvres d'art que prodigue ce pays s'il n'y avait la façon d'être désinvolte des italiens, qui vivent tout naturellement avec ces témoignages de leur histoire plus de deux fois millénaire.

Les hôtels présentés dans cet ouvrage reflètent cette coexistence passionnante, tant dans des métropoles telles que Milan, Florence ou Rome, que dans les régions de l'intérieur ou les îles. On peut prendre comme exemple le *Falconara Charming Resort* au sud de la Sicile, un hôtel de vacances moderne construit par le Baron Bordonaro, avec vue sur son majestueux *castello* médiéval. Le nouvel hôtel se réfère subtilement à la forteresse défensive au bord de la mer. Un autre exemple en est le *Castello del Nero*, une résidence nobiliaire du XIIème siècle, située entre Sienne et Florence, qui dispose de suites luxueuses dans lesquelles on peut se reposer entouré de fresques authentiques.

Tout en haut des falaises abruptes de la côte d'Amalfi, où l'on peut encore ressentir une certaine atmosphère glamour des années 50, se situe la *Casa Angelina*, d'une blancheur resplendissante et dont les formes cubistes dénotent un caractère contemporain marqué. La vue spectaculaire sur la mer Tyrrhénienne et la côte escarpée dont on jouit depuis la terrasse et le vestibule vaut le détour. La *Casa della Palma* et le *Daphne Inn*, deux B&B qui offrent un confort abordable dans une atmosphère élégante, prouvent que séjourner à Rome n'est pas forcément cher. A l'autre bout de la gamme, l'ouverture du *Bulgari Hotel* à Milan, qui rend hommage à cette métropole internationale de la mode et du design, a ouvert la voie à d'autres hôtels comme le *NHow-Hotel*, *The Chedi Milan*, *The Gray* et le *STRAF*. Ce dernier représente une sorte de provocation de Vincenzo de Cotiis, architecte et créateur de mode, qui a employé des matériaux habituellement utilisés uniquement dans la fabrication industrielle, pour créer un hôtel de luxe derrière la façade d'un ancien palazzo.

Bärbel Holzberg

Introducción

Partir de viaje a Italia causa mayor efecto que el propio inicio de las vacaciones. Siempre implica el deseo de encontrar otra actitud ante la vida, esa alegría de vivir y de disfrutar con tranquilidad propias del Mediterráneo. Posiblemente sea Italia el destino turístico más valorado en el mundo. Imágenes como la de los paisajes toscanos de suaves colinas de olivos con destellos argénteos y de atractivos cipreses en tonos oscuros crean adicción, no menos que las escarpadas y silvestres áreas del sur, que en algunas zonas de Cerdeña, Sicilia y Apulia llegan a resultar arcaicas. Cabría rendirse ante la abundancia de obras de arte que atesora este país, algo que no llega a producirse gracias a la despreocupada forma de ser de los italianos, que conviven con toda naturalidad con estos testigos de sus más de dos mil años de historia.

Los hoteles presentados en el presente volumen reflejan esa interesante forma de convivencia tanto en metrópolis como Milán, Florencia o Roma, como en las regiones del interior o en las islas. Valga como ejemplo el *Falconara Charming Resort* al sur de Sicilia, un moderno hotel vacacional levantado por el barón Bordonaro, hotel que el barón alcanza a divisar desde su grandioso *castello* medieval. El nuevo hotel cuenta con sutiles referencias a la fortificación defensiva al borde del mar. Otro ejemplo es el *Castello del Nero*, residencia nobiliaria del siglo XII ubicada entre Siena y Florencia, y que cuenta con lujosas *suites* en las que descansar rodeado de frescos auténticos.

En lo alto de los abruptos acantilados de la costa de Amalfi, en la que aún se respira cierto aire glamuroso propio de los años 50, se sitúa *Casa Angelina*, de un blancor resplandeciente y unas formas claramente cubistas, que denotan un marcado carácter contemporáneo. Aunque tan solo fuera por las espectaculares vistas al Tirreno y a su escarpada costa que se disfrutan desde la terraza y el vestíbulo, merece la pena viajar hasta allí. Que los hoteles en Roma no tienen por qué ser necesariamente caros lo demuestran la *Casa della Palma* y el *Daphne Inn*, dos B&B que ofrecen un nivel de confort más que razonable en un ambiente muy estilizado. Por su parte, la inauguración del *Bulgari Hotel* en Milán, ciudad considerada con todo merecimiento el centro internacional de la moda y del diseño, supuso el pistoletazo de salida para la apertura de otros hoteles como el *NHow-Hotel*, el *The Chedi Milan*, el *The Gray* y el *STRAF*. Este último supone toda una provocación por parte de Vincenzo de Cotiis, arquitecto y diseñador de moda, al haber empleado materiales habituales únicamente en la construcción industrial, y todo ello en un hotel de lujo tras la fachada de un antiguo *palazzo*.

Bärbel Holzberg

La Sommità

Via Scipione Petrarolo 7
72017 Ostuni
Apulia
Phone: +39 08 31 30 59 25
Fax: +39 08 31 30 67 29
www.lasommita.it

Price category: €€€
Rooms: 4 deluxe rooms, 3 junior suites, 3 suites
Facilities: Restaurant, wine bar, spa
Services: Internet, shop, laundry, free parking area
Located: in the historical center of Ostuni, the white town, 100 km to Bari airport and 45 km to Brindisi airport
Map: No. 1
Style: Modern
What's special: In what feels like someone's wonderfully decorated, relaxing home, La Sommità provides a kind of grace only found in the finest private residences in Italy. Fresh local food is served under the massive vaulted ceiling in the restaurant.

Casa Angelina

Via G. Capriglione 147
84010 Praiano, Almafi Coast
Campania
Phone: +39 08 98 13 13 33
Fax: +39 08 98 74 266
www.steinhotels.com/
casaangelina

Price category: €€
Rooms: 40 rooms and suites
Facilities: Restaurant "Un piano nel cielo", lobby bar, panorama terrace, pool, wellness, sauna, private beach
Services: Space for private events for up to 120 people
Located: in a small town located on the Amalfi Coast, between Amalfi and Positano, 60 km to Naples airport
Map: No. 2
Style: Minimalistic
What's special: With sweeping views of the sea and a charming, rustic vibe, Casa Angelina is a Mediterranean favorite. The swimming pool has a counter current and the ceilings of its world famous spa have fiber optic lights that suggest the appearance of a star filled sky.

duoMo hotel & noMi club

Via Giordano Bruno 28
47900 Rimini
Emilia Romagna
Phone: +39 0541 24 215/6
Fax: +39 0541 27 842
www.duomohotel.com

Price category: €
Rooms: 23 urban rooms, 11 loop rooms and 9 dreaming suites
Facilities: noMi club & "noMi al duoMo" Restaurant
Services: WiFi internet access, babysitting, clubbing, city bikes, conference rooms
Located: in the historical city center, 900 meters to the beach and 400 meters to train station
Map: No. 3
Style: Contemporary design
What's special: Designed by superstar architect Ron Arad, the striking hotel features a retro-futuristic lobby with a gigantic chrome ring shaped front desk resembling a donut. Guests receive use of a bicycle and get free welcome drink for the noMi club.

Hotel Carducci76

Via Carducci 76
47841 Cattolica
Emilia Romagna
Phone: +39 05 41 95 46 77
Fax: +39 05 41 83 15 57
www.carducci76.it

Price category: €€
Rooms: 35 rooms and 3 suites
Facilities: "Ristorante Vicolo Santa Lucia", bar, garden, pool
Located: directly on the beach
Map: No. 4
Style: Minimalistic
What's special: Owned by the brother of fashion designer Alberta Ferretti, this 38-room hotel is a stylish, yet understated boutique property. Located in a converted 1920s ocean front villa, the light, modern furnishings and sun drenched rooms give it an air of breezy elegance. "Ristorante Vicolo Santa Lucia" is a local favorite.

Sixty Hotel

Via Milano 54
47838 Riccione, Rimini
Emilia Romagna
Phone: +39 05 41 69 78 51
Fax: +39 05 41 47 55 40
www.sixtyhotel.com

Price category: €€
Rooms: 39 rooms
Facilities: Bar, terrace, 24-hour front desk, non-smoking rooms, facilities for disabled guests, elevator, express check-in/check-out, soundproofed rooms, heating, luggage storage, shops
Services: High speed internet access, WiFi
Located: next to the beach of Riccione, 2-minutes walk to main station, 10 km to Rimini airport
Map: No. 5
Style: Contemporary design
What's special: Each room is a unique piece of art, having been decorated by the world's hottest up and coming artists. The façade changes every night, often lit up with light shows and video art commissioned just for the hotel.

UNA Hotel Bologna

Viale Pietramellara 41/43
40121 Bologna
Emilia Romagna
Phone: +39 05 16 08 01
Fax: +39 05 16 08 02
www.unahotels.it

Price category: €€
Rooms: 93 rooms and 6 residential suites
Facilities: Patio bar, restaurant, 3 meeting rooms
Services: WiFi internet access in common areas and meeting rooms, hi-speed connection in the rooms
Located: in the center of Bologna, in front of the railway station
Map: No. 6
Style: Contemporary design
What's special: Like something out of Star Trek, the glossy black lobby features embedded flat screen televisions and futuristic furnishings. This hotel has six private apartments for longer staying guests. The UNAthletic rooms are provided with exercise equipment so guests can work out where they sleep.

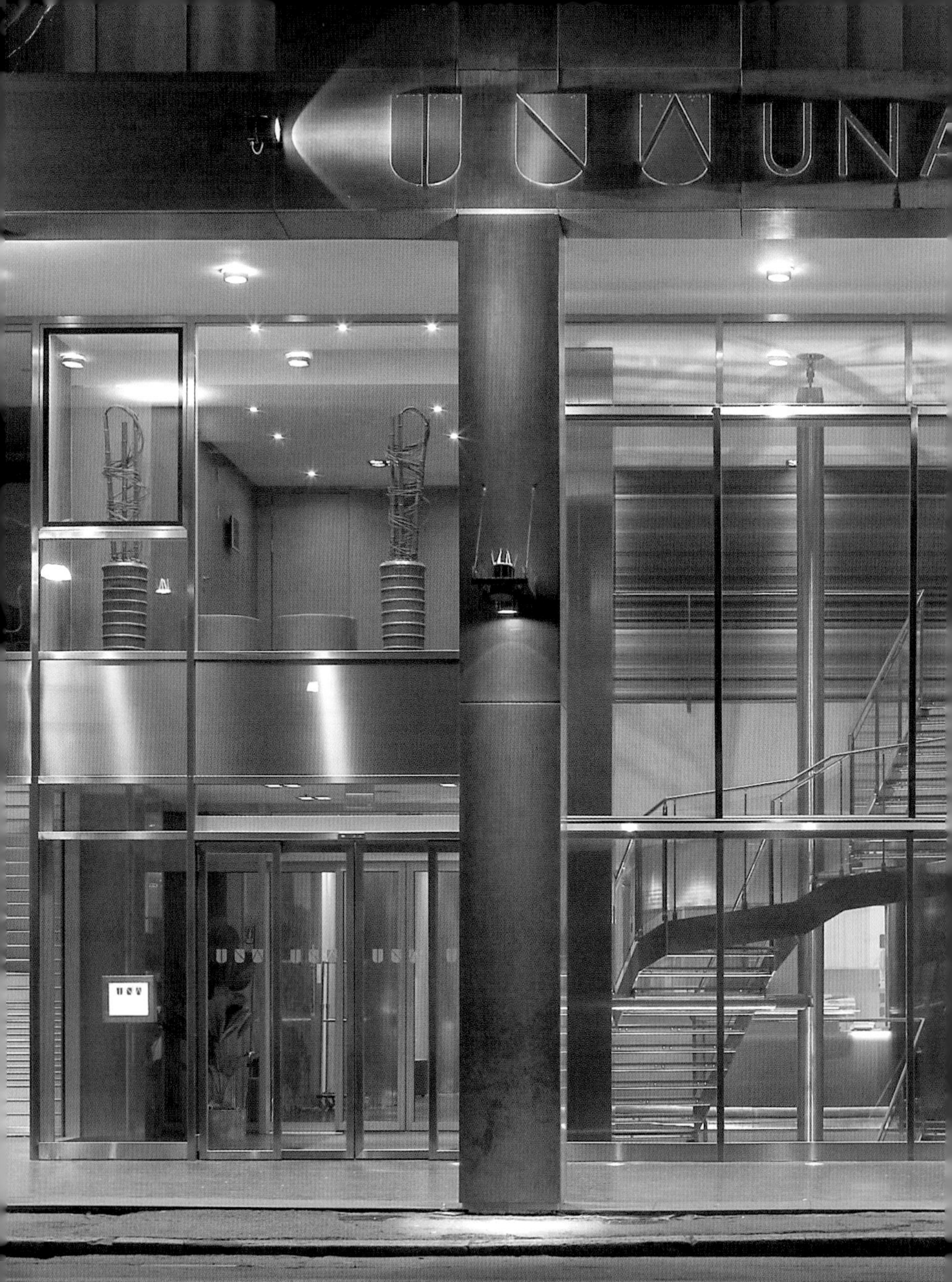
UNA
UNA

Continentale

Vicolo dell'Oro 6r
50123 Florence
Tuscany
Phone: +39 055 27 26 40 00
Fax: +39 055 27 26 44 44
www.lungarnohotels.com

Price category: €€€
Rooms: 43 rooms including 1 penthouse suite
Facilities: Bar, rooftop lounge, fitness center
Located: in the center of Florence, next to Ponte Vecchio
Map: No. 7
Style: Contemporary design
What's special: The unbeatable location just above the Arno sets the tone in this much loved hotel. The pale décor, offset by the striking black and white photography creates a modern feel. Home theater room, rooftop lounge and fitness center with sauna are additional modern assets of this hotel.

J.K. Place

Piazza Santa Maria Novella 7
50123 Florence
Tuscany
Phone: +39 055 26 45 181
Fax: +39 055 26 58 387
www.jkplace.com

Price category: €€€
Rooms: 20 rooms and suites
Facilities: J.K. bar and restaurant, lounge restaurant, rooftop terrace
Located: at Piazza Santa Maria Novella, just a few steps from the Renaissance church bearing the same name
Map: No. 8
Style: Contemporary Italian design
What's special: Staying at this small hotel is akin to spending the night at the home of an elegant friend; the staff is friendly, the feeling is warm, and the understated beauty of the rooms and lobby feels inviting, never stuffy. The rooftop terrace features year round lounging options.

Riva Lofts Florence

Via Baccio Bandinelli 98
50142 Florence
Tuscany
Phone: +39 055 71 30 272
Fax: +39 055 71 11 03
www.rivalofts.com

Price category: €€
Rooms: 9 studios with independent entrance
Facilities: "Honesty Bar", outdoor pool, 24/7 living room
Services: Massages and babysitting on request,
concierge and bikes available for guests
Located: along the Arno, opposite of Parco delle Cascine
Map: No. 9
Style: Contemporary design
What's special: Pure and contemporary. The warm atmosphere in these distinctive spaces is due to an accurate balance amongst modern antiques, as 1950s furniture, old and new materials as wood and corian, and examples of sophisticated design as the kitchens designed by Claudio Nardi.

Via Pisana 59
50143 Florence
Tuscany
Phone: +39 055 22 771
Fax: +39 055 22 772
www.unahotels.it

Price category: €€
Rooms: 82 rooms
Facilities: American bar, restaurant, indoor parking space
Services: 3 meeting rooms, WiFi internet access in common areas and meeting rooms, high speed internet connection in all rooms
Located: in the center of Florence, 1.5 km to central station, 8 km to Florence airport
Map: No. 10
Style: Modern classic
What's special: Though it may look like a disco, UNA Hotel Vittoria is a great place to spend time in the city. Rooms feature black/fuchsia lacquer wall with ultimate lighting system varying colors, crystal bathrooms and a reception area entirely covered in a fabulous floral mosaic.

Palazzo Arzaga Hotel Spa & Golf Resort

Carzago di Calvagese della Riviera
25080 Brescia
Lombardy
Phone: +39 030 68 06 00
Fax: +39 030 68 06 270
www.palazzoarzaga.com

Price category: €€€
Rooms: 80 rooms, 4 suites
Facilities: Italian restaurant "Il Moretto", "Enoteca" bar, spa, pools, golf course and a lot of sport activities
Services: Conference rooms
Located: in the midst of green landscape, 45 km to Verona Catullo Airport
Map: No. 11
Style: Italian elegance
What's special: Features a full regimen for weight loss, health and beauty custom designed for each guest. Rooms are individually decorated with ancient frescoes.

Alle Meraviglie

Via San Tomaso 8
20121 Milan
Centro Storico
Phone: +39 02 80 51 023
Fax: +39 02 80 54 090
www.allemeraviglie.it

Price category: €€
Rooms: 10 rooms
Facilities: Patio
Services: Fresh flowers, internet access
Located: in the historical center of Milan
Public transportation: Metro Cordusio, Duomo
Map: No. 12
Style: Cozy and charming
What's special: The epitome of understated elegance, this small boutique hotel is decorated in a whimsical interplay between old and new. The name of the hotel means "wonderland" and it certainly lives up to that: unexpected touches of color surprise guests around every corner.

Bulgari Hotel Milan

Via Privata Fratelli Gabba 7b
20121 Milan
Brera
Phone: +39 02 80 58 051
Fax: +39 02 80 58 05 222
www.bulgarihotels.com

Price category: €€€€
Rooms: 58 rooms and suites
Facilities: Restaurant and bar, lounge, indoor pool, spa, hammam, fitness center, garden, wellness area
Services: Personal shopper, hair and make up service, 24-h valet parking, complimentary packing and unpacking service
Located: in the heart of Milan, next to the botanical garden
Public transportation: Metro Monte Napoleone
Map: No. 13
Style: Contemporary design
What's special: As one might expect from the famous brand, the hotel is the embodiment of the cool passion that typifies Italian design. The surrounding gardens are a favorite place for Milanese to go chill out.

Via Tortona 35
20144 Milan
Tortona-Navigli
Phone: +39 02 48 98 861
Fax: +39 02 48 98 86 489
www.nhow-hotels.com

Price category: €€€
Rooms: 246 rooms, including 135 superior rooms, 23 junior suites, 6 suites, 1 penthouse
Facilities: Bar, restaurant, spa
Services: Meeting facilities for up to 1.300 people
Located: in the Tortona-Navigli area, between the inner and the outer ring roads surrounding the city center
Public transportation: Metro Porta Genova
Map: No. 14
Style: Minimalistic
What's special: Reborn from the ashes of a once-industrial district, NHow-Hotel is among the most talked about design hotels in the world. Rooms are functionally chic, and are anchored by a dramatic lobby in glass, steel, and wood.

Via San Raffaele 3
20121 Milan
Centro Storico
Phone: +39 02 80 50 81
Fax: +39 02 89 09 52 94
www.straf.it

Price category: €€
Rooms: 64 rooms, including 2 suites and 1 executive room with private terrace
Facilities: Bar STRAF, fitness room, relax rooms
Services: High-speed internet access, LCD TV, satellite TV, safe, music, room service
Located: close to Duomo, La Scala Opera House, Vittorio Emanuele Gallery II and Montenapoleone Street
Public transportation: Metro Duomo
Map: No. 15
Style: Combination of minimalist design and classic Italian architecture
What's special: Inspired by a quintessentially Italian fusion of functionality and fashion, STRAF features bold modern art, with the 64 rooms and suites blending design and functionality, maximizing comfort.

Via Villapizzone 24
20156 Milan
Bovisa
Phone: +39 02 36 31 888
Fax: +39 02 36 31 870
www.thechedimilan.com

Price category: €€
Rooms: 290 rooms and suites, including The Penthouse on 10th floor with terrace and 40 rooms for long stays
Facilities: The Bar, The Restaurant (Italian, Indian and Thai cuisine), The Conference Centre, the spa "Institut Dominique Chenot", The Chedi Club on 6th floor
Services: Shuttle to center, butler service
Located: in Bovisa district, 15-minutes taxi drive to center
Public transportation: Tram 12, bus 57, Passante S5+S6
Map: No. 16
Style: Urban chic
What's special: If an Italian opened a hotel in Indonesia, it would look like The Chedi. The Asian inspired décor, in a minimalist palette of cool browns and grays is instantly relaxing. The Asian-Southern European fusion restaurant is off of the lobby.

The Gray

Via San Raffaele 6
20121 Milan
Centro Storico
Phone: +39 02 72 08 951
Fax: +39 02 86 65 26
www.hotelthegray.com

Price category: €€€
Rooms: 21 rooms and suites
Facilities: "Le Noir" restaurant, The "GBar"
Services: WiFi internet access, meeting room
Located: between the dome of Milan and La Scala
Public transportation: Metro Duomo
Map: No. 17
Style: Fashionista
What's special: From the moment you step foot in the lobby and see the pink mattress suspended from the ceiling, you know you're somewhere special. Some suites have private workout rooms and still others have private steam rooms.

Town House Galleria

Via Silvio Pellico 8
20121 Milan
Centro Storico
Phone: +39 02 89 05 82 97
Fax: +39 02 89 05 82 99
www.townhousegalleria.it

Price category: €€€€
Rooms: 24 rooms and suites
Facilities: Bar, restaurant "La Sinfonia" (only for guests)
Services: Exclusive butler service, events planning, shopping and art planning
Located: in the heart of Milan, inside the historical Galleria Vittorio Emanuele II
Public transportation: Metro 1, 3 Duomo
Map: No. 18
Style: Rustic elegance
What's special: It is the only hotel inside the historical Galleria Vittorio Emanuele II built in 1876 and the ultimate luxury destination in Milan with interior design by architect Ettore Mocchetti. There is a butler assigned to every room.

Townhouse 12

Piazza Gerusalemme 12
20154 Milan
Zona Corso Sempione
Telefon: +39 02 89 07 85 11
Fax: +39 02 89 07 85 17
www.townhouse.it

Price category: €€€
Rooms: 18 rooms
Facilities: Terrace bar and lobby bar
Services: Meeting room
Located: close to the trade fair
Public transportation: Tram Cenisio/Borgese and Procaccini/Lomazzo
Map: No. 19
Style: Minimalistic
What's special: From the outside, this hotel may seem too simple, but it is its minimalism that makes it so glamorous. The rooms are decorated in muted gray and black, and the lobby bar, "T" is a great place to watch the beautiful people come and go.

Via di San Basilio 15
00187 Rome
Centro Storico
Phone: +39 06 42 29 01
Fax: +39 06 42 29 00 00
www.boscolohotels.com

Price category: €€€€
Rooms: 96 rooms including 24 deluxe rooms and
6 suites and junior suites
Facilities: Restaurant "Sin", bar, rooftop terrace, library,
spa with sauna, turkish bath and thermal swimming pool
Located: next to the Via Veneto
Public transportation: Metro Barberini
Map: No. 20
Style: Glamorous
What's special: The hotel itself is a piece of art. Exceptionally designed, it features Murano glass chandeliers, a beautiful roof terrace with sweeping views of Rome, and an indoor swimming pool. The interiors are based on Dante's Inferno.

Casa della Palma

Via dei Sabelli 98
00185 Rome
San Lorenzo
Phone: +39 06 44 54 264
Fax: +39 06 23 32 45 562
www.casadellapalma.it

Price category: €
Rooms: 8 rooms and loft for 5 people
Facilities: Rooftop terrace, green inner courtyard
Services: Free city bikes, internet access in all rooms
Located: in the trendy San Lorenzo district
Public transportation: Tram Reti, Bus Marrucini
Map: No. 21
Style: Romantic-industrial
What's special: This townhouse-style hotel feels like a comfortable private home, with rooms decorated individually in a classic style. Bicycles are available for use by guests. The outdoor terrace is great for relaxation.

Via di San Basilio 55
00187 Rome
Centro Storico
Phone: +39 06 87 45 00 86/7
Fax: +39 06 23 32 40 967
www.daphne-rome.com

Price category: €
Rooms: 8 rooms
Facilities: All rooms have private bathrooms (although two of the rooms' private bathrooms are outside their respective rooms)
Services: Mobile phone with important numbers, personalized concierge and trip-planning help
Located: in the historic center of Rome, just a few minutes away from the Trevi Fountain
Public transportation: Metro Barberini
Map: No. 22
Style: Modern, minimalist yet warm, with ethnic touches
What's special: Fresh fruits and pastries are complimentary every morning. Guests receive use of a cell phone during their stay. Rooms are spacious and well appointed.

Exedra

Piazza della Repubblica 47
00187 Rome
Centro Storico
Phone: +39 06 48 93 81
Fax: +39 06 48 93 87 77
www.boscolohotels.com

Price category: €€€€
Rooms: 240 rooms, including 11 junior suites, 3 suites, 3 executive suites and 1 presidential suite
Facilities: 2 exclusive restaurants, rooftop terrace with infinity pool
Services: Modern business center
Located: in the center of Rome near the Piazza della Repubblica and Basilica degli Angeli
Public transportation: Metro Repubblica
Map: No. 23
Style: Luxury elegance
What's special: The large rooms here are sumptuously decorated in marble, wood, and glass. Breakfast is served on the rooftop terrace that overlooks Fountain of the Naiads. The spa features a private glass elevator.

Fortyseven

Via Petroselli 47
00186 Rome
Campidoglio
Phone: +39 06 67 87 816
Fax: +39 06 69 19 07 26
www.fortysevenhotel.com

Price category: €€
Rooms: 61 rooms
Facilities: Rooftop restaurant, bar
Services: All rooms have internet access, meeting rooms for up to 50 people
Located: in the heart of ancient Rome, between Circo Massimo and Mouth of the Truth
Public transportation: Metro Circo Massimo
Map: No. 24
Style: Mixture of modern style and timeless Art Deco
What's special: Each floor is decorated according to a different Italian artist: Mastroianni, Greco, Modigliani, Quagliata, and Guccione. The Art Deco style of the rooms, and the great amenities including a full gym and spa with Turkish bath, make this one of Rome's best.

Hotel Aldrovandi Palace

Via Ulisse Aldrovandi 15
00197 Rome
Villa Borghese
Phone: +39 06 32 23 993
Fax: +39 06 32 21 435
www.aldrovandi.com

Price category: €€€€
Rooms: 108 rooms including 16 suites
Facilities: Restaurant "baby", poolbar, outdoor pool and fitness
Services: Shuttle service to Via Veneto and Spanish Steps, conference and banquet rooms for up to 300 people
Located: directly a the Villa Borghese gardens
Public transportation: Tram Aldrovandi
Map: No. 25
Style: Luxury elegance
What's special: Built in the spirit of the ancient Roman palaces, the hotel has its own private park, outdoor pool and garden dining in the Michelin-starred restaurant. The elegance and unique style of the hotel is enhanced by the recent refurbishment of the lobby and the rooms.

Hotel de Russie

Via del Babuino 9
00187 Rome
Piazza del Popolo
Phone: +39 06 32 88 81
Fax: +39 06 32 88 88 88
www.hotelderussie.it

Price category: €€€€
Rooms: 122 rooms including 34 suites
Facilities: Restaurant, bar, De Russie Wellness Zone with hydropool, jacuzzi, sauna, Turkish steam bath, beauty treatments and gym
Services: 4 meeting rooms for up to 90 people
Located: between the Spanish Steps and Piazza del Popolo
Public transportation: Metro Flaminio–Piazza del Popolo
Map: No. 26
Style: Essential
What's special: Features a beautiful courtyard, a Butterfly Oasis in terraced gardens that run up the Pincio hill. The De Russie Wellness Zone is equipped with a saltwater whirlpool and personal trainers.

St. George Roma

Via Giulia 62
00186 Rome
Center
Phone: +39 06 68 66 11
Fax: +39 06 68 66 12 30
www.stgeorgehotel.it

Price category: €€€
Rooms: 64 rooms
Facilities: Restaurant "I Sofà di Via Giulia", "Terrazza Rosé" roof terrace, wine bar, spa with whirlpool, sauna, turkish bath, hydro massage, personalized treatments and gym with cardio-fitness equipment, library
Services: High-speed internet, full concierge service, limousine service, butler on request
Located: in the historical center of Rome
Public transportation: Electric bus N° 116
Map: No. 27
Style: Contemporary design
What's special: Featuring a wine bar, starred restaurant and cigar lounge. There is a world class spa with sauna and Turkish bath. The main terrace offers unparalleled views of Rome.

Cala di Volpe

Costa Smeralda
07020 Porto Cervo
Sardinia
Phone: +39 07 89 97 61 11
Fax: +39 07 89 97 66 17
www.luxurycollection.com/
caladivolpe

Price category: €€€€
Rooms: 125 rooms and suites each with balcony
Facilities: Gourmet restaurant, bar, saltwater swimming pool
Services: Boat rentals, fitness, tennis, water sports
Located: in the north-east of Sardinia
Map: No. 28
Style: Traditional elements
What's special: Spacious rooms and sweeping views make this one of Europe's best resort hotels. The restaurant serves fresh seafood. The large saltwater pool is popular in the warm months.

La Coluccia

Località Conca Verde
07028 Santa Teresa Gallura
Sardinia
Phone: +39 0789 75 80 04
www.lacoluccia.it

Price category: €€
Rooms: 45 rooms
Facilities: Restaurant, bar
Located: directly at a private beach
Map: No. 29
Style: Contemporary design
What's special: This property, created by architect Alvin Grassi, is a water-lovers dream. On the private beach, guests are given towels, sun loungers, and sunshades. The outdoor swimming pool is just steps away.

Spiagge Sanpietro Resort

Strada prov. 18 km 14,200
San Pietro Marina
09040 Castiadas
Sardinia
Phone: +39 070 99 59 30
www.mobygest.it

Price category: €€
Rooms: 110 rooms with patio or balcony
Facilities: Bar, restaurant, boutique, main swimming pool with bar, children's pool, two tennis courts
Services: Amphitheater for evening entertainment
Located: next to the white sandy beach at the South East coast of Sardinia, 65 km to Cagliari
Map: No. 30
Style: Minimalistic
What's special: The clean white rooms and pristine beach, coupled with an exclusive mineral and thermal spa make this island resort, created by Alvin Grassi, one of the best in the region.

Via Elorina 154,
Contrada Pantanelli
96100 Syracuse
Sicily
Phone: +39 09 31 69 057
Fax: +39 09 31 68 561
www.caolishka.com

Price category: €€
Rooms: 10 rooms
Facilities: "Zafferano" Restaurant, garden, swimming pool, massages
Services: WiFi, excursions, sailing
Located: next to a natural reserve, 2 km to Syracuse's old town
Map: No. 31
Style: Mixture of modern and Sicilian design
What's special: This incredibly designed hotel, combines old world with new. Filled with contemporary furniture, and state-of-the-art electronics, the buildings once housed an old barn. The cuisine is nouvelle-Sicilian.

Donnalucata Resort Sicily

Strada provinciale 63 km 3 loc.
Donnalucata
97010 Scicli
Sicily
Phone: +39 0932 85 02 85
www.hotelphilosophy.net

Price category: €
Rooms: 105 rooms
Facilities: Restaurant with terrace, pool bar, swimming pool, private beach
Services: Babysitting
Located: next to the beach
Map: No. 32
Style: Contemporary design
What's special: Made almost entirely of native stone, this special place, created by Alvin Grassi, feels like something from another time. The interior courtyard provides a backdrop for warm romantic evenings. The restaurant features authentic Sicilian cuisine. The beach is private.

Falconara Charming House & Resort

Strada statale 215 km
243 Falconara
93011 Butera
Sicily
Phone: +39 0934 34 90 12
www.mobygest.it

Price category: €€
Rooms: 70 rooms
Facilities: Restaurant, bar, spa, private beach
Services: Babysitting
Located: directly at the sea
Map: No. 33
Style: Contemporary design
What's special: Built on a private beach, this luxury boutique property is a secret gem on the coast. Rooms are well appointed, with black stone floors and marble tubs.

Santa Teresa Resort

Via Contrada Monastero Alto-Sibà
91010 Scauri Siculo, Pantelleria
Sicily
Phone: +39 0923 91 63 89
www.hotelphilosophy.net

Price category: €
Rooms: 18 bungalows
Facilities: Swimming pools, gardens, health treatments
Located: in the village of Sibà, 10 km away from Pantelleria center and 8 km to the local airport
Map: No. 34
Style: Contemporary design
What's special: Comprised of 18 "dammusi" (bungalows) that are arranged in four mini-villages, each decorated differently in a fusion of African, Mediterranean and Italian styles. Guests relax each evening in an Arabian style garden.

Hotel Greif

Waltherplatz
(Entrance Raingasse)
39100 Bolzano
South Tyrol
Phone: +39 0471 31 80 00
Fax: +39 0471 31 81 48
www.greif.it

Price category: €
Rooms: 33 rooms, each furnished by an artist
Facilities: Garden restaurant, "Laurin" Bar with piano music, Lounge Bar "Grifoncino" (opened 2007)
Services: Meeting and banquet facilities
Located: in the historical center of Bolzano, in walking distance to the main station, 10-minutes drive to the airport
Map: No. 35
Style: Contemporary design
What's special: Built in an historical building, each reconstructed room features two original art works; one by a renowned artist and another by a young up and coming artist. The hotel is located in a quiet pedestrian area.

vigilius mountain resort

Mount S. Vigilius
39011 Lana
South Tyrol
Phone +39 0473 55 66 00
Fax: +39 0473 55 66 99
www.vigilius.it

Price category: €€€
Rooms: 35 rooms and 6 suites
Facilities: 2 restaurants, library, yoga room, boccia court
Services: move & explore (free activity program),
Five Tibetan, archery, shiatsu & watsu, wine tasting, yoga
Located: 1500 meter above sea level, reached only by
cable car, 8 km to Meran
Map: No. 36
Style: Ecological contemporary design
What's special: There are film screenings each night
in the library. The grounds feature quartzite-lined indoor
pools and outdoor sundecks. Archery and yoga are avail-
able for guests.

Castello del Nero Hotel & Spa

Strada di Spicciano 7 – C.P. 36
50028 Tavarnelle V.P.
Tuscany
Phone: +39 055 80 64 70
Fax: +39 055 80 64 77 77
www.castellodelnero.com

Price category: €€€€
Rooms: 50 rooms and suites
Facilities: "La Torre" Restaurant, The Bar, ESPA, 2 tennis courts
Services: High speed internet, shuttle bus from\to center of Florence
Located: in the heart of the Chianti wine region, 25-minutes drive to Florence and Siena
Map: No. 37
Style: Italian luxury
What's special: The hotel restaurant, "La Torre", serves fresh and authentic Tuscan gourmet food and wine and has some of the best views in the region. Hot air balloon rides, private gym, and heated swimming pool are available.

Granducato

Via Di Tomerello 1
50013 Campi Di Bisenzio
Tuscany
Phone: +39 05 58 80 51 11
Fax: +39 05 58 80 50 00
www.boscolohotels.com

Price category: €€€€
Rooms: 60 rooms and suites
Facilities: Restaurant, brasserie, garden, pool, fitness room, private chapel
Services: Conference rooms, shuttle service
Located: in green landscape, 15 km to the city center of Florence, 5 km to Prato
Map: No. 38
Style: Mixture of original architecture and modern furnishing
What's special: Once an orphanage, this hotel sits on beautifully manicured grounds in the heart of the Tuscan countryside. Many of the guestrooms contain the original 16th century architecture, but have been updated with chic, contemporary furnishings.

Villa Fontelunga

Via Cunicchio 5
Loc. Pozzo, Foiano della Chiana
52045 Arezzo
Tuscany
Phone: +39 0575 66 04 10
Fax: +39 0575 66 19 63
www.fontelunga.com

Price category: €€
Rooms: 8 rooms
Facilities: Swimming pool
Services: Dinner parties
Located: in the heart of Tuscany surrounded by the typical Tuscan countryside
Map: No. 39
Style: Mixture of modern and ancient elements
What's special: Guests eat communally by candlelight in the warm months. Mountain bikes are available. The outdoor pool is nestled amongst an olive grove.

Ca' Nigra Lagoon Resort

Campo di San Simeon Grande 927
30135 Venice
Santa Croce
Phone: +39 041 27 50 047
Fax: +39 041 24 48 721
www.hotelcanigra.com

Price category: €€€
Rooms: 22 junior suites
Facilities: Bar (in the rose garden at Canal Grande), boat garage
Services: WiFi internet access
Located: directly at Canal Grande
Public transportation: Vaporetto Riva di Biasio
Map: No. 40
Style: Modern luxury
What's special: Located on the most important waterway in Venice, the Canal Grande, Ca' Nigra Lagoon Resort mixes the charm of an old palazzo with contemporary furnishings and art. The bathrooms are huge.

Ca' Pozzo

Sottoportico Ca' Pozzo 1279
30121 Venice
Cannaregio
Phone: +34 041 52 40 504
Fax: +34 041 52 44 099
www.capozzovenice.com

Price category: €€
Rooms: 15 rooms
Facilities: Patio, garden, terrace
Services: Ticket service
Located: next to Ponte delle Guglie in the ancient Jewish Ghetto of Venice
Public transportation: Vaporetto Guglie
Map: No. 41
Style: Minimalistic
What's special: The beautiful interior courtyard attracts guests throughout the day. A constantly changing contemporary art collection adorns the walls. Guest rooms are relaxed and modern.

San Marco 1332
30124 Venice
San Marco
Phone: +39 041 52 00 211
Fax: +39 041 52 00 501
www.hotelmonaco.it

Price category: €€€
Rooms: 100 rooms
Facilities: "Grand Canal Restaurant" with terrace (famous Venetian cuisine with fresh ingredients from Italy), bar
Services: Conference rooms for up to 250 people, gala dinner for up to 600 people
Located: in the center of Venice, overlooking the Canal Grande
Public transportation: Vaporetto Valaresso
Map: No. 42
Style: Mixture of contemporary design and antiques
What's special: A stunning mix of Baroque splendor and sleek contemporary design, the hotel features the Antico Ridotto Publico room, which was the site of the world's first casino in 1638 and houses today the conference and dinner facilities, and 8 more halls.

Novecento

Calle del Dose
Campo San Maurizio 2683/84
30124 Venice
San Marco
Phone: +39 041 24 13 765
Fax: +39 041 52 12 145
www.novecento.biz

Price category: €€
Rooms: 9 rooms
Facilities: Patio
Services: Art exhibitions in the hotel
Located: between Piazza San Marco and the Accademia Gallery
Public transportation: Vaporetto Santa Maria del Giglio
Map: No. 43
Style: Elegance
What's special: This cozy courtyard invites you to relax and enjoy the atmosphere of Venice. Rooms are decorated in soft, muted colors and inspire relaxation and peace. The hotel is family owned and run.

Oltre il Giardino

Fondamenta Contarini
San Polo 2542
30125 Venice
San Polo
Phone: +39 041 27 50 015
Fax: +39 041 79 54 52
www.oltreilgiardino-venezia.com

Price category: €€
Rooms: 6 rooms
Facilities: Garden
Services: High speed internet access, baby sitting on request, satellite TV
Located: in the heart of Venice, next to the Church of the Frari and the Scuola Grande di S.Rocco in a quiet and historical area, 15-minutes walk to Rialto Bridge
Public transportation: Public boat transport, water taxi
Map: No. 44
Style: Italian elegance
What's special: The stylish, classic rooms are decorated with Edwardian art and family heirlooms. In the evenings, guests lounge in oversized sofas sipping complimentary drinks.

Byblos Art Hotel Villa Amistà

Via Cedrare 78
37029 Verona
Corrubbio di Negarine
Phone: +39 045 68 55 555
Fax: +39 045 68 55 500
www.byblosarthotel.com

Price category: €€€
Rooms: 60 rooms
Facilities: Gourmet restaurant, bar and spa
Located: in the middle of a park in the Valpolicella area, 7 km to the center of Verona
Map: No. 45
Style: Contemporary design mixed with art
Special features: Run by the Byblos fashion empire, this hotel boasts the best collection of contemporary furniture and art of any hotel in the world. The Henri & Dominique Chenot spa offers treatments in a tile-lined building.

2004: 24 HOURS NIGHT (TELL ME, WHERE THE COLOURS HAVE GONE???)

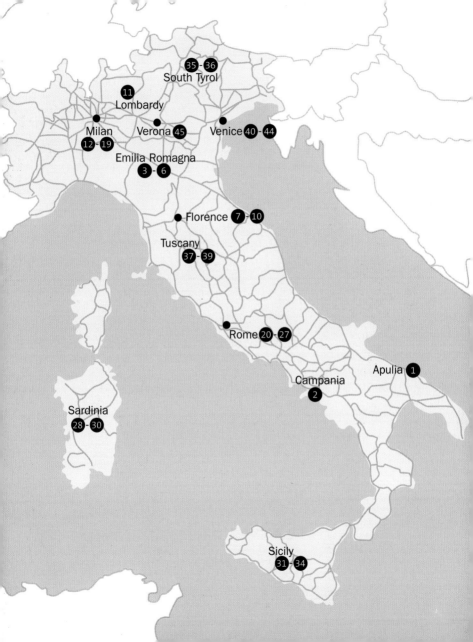

Other titles by teNeues

Styleguides

ISBN 978-3-8327-9206-0

ISBN 978-3-8327-9207-7

ISBN 978-3-8327-9205-3

ISBN 978-3-8327-9234-3

ISBN 978-3-8327-9230-5

ISBN 978-3-8327-9243-5

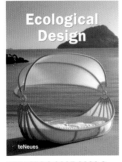

ISBN 978-3-8327-9229-9

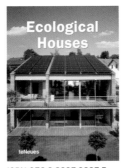

ISBN 978-3-8327-9227-5

ISBN 978-3-8327-9228-2

Size: **15 x 19 cm**, 6 x 7 ½ in., 224 pp., **Flexicover**, c. 280 color photographs,
Text: English / German / French / Spanish / Italian
www.teneues.com